Catholic Quick View

Second Edition

Catholic Quick View
Second Edition

beliefs · definitions · prayers · practices
symbols · saints

Brian Singer-Towns,
Marilyn Kielbasa
Robert Feduccia Jr.

saint mary's press

Nihil Obstat: Rev. Andrew Beerman, STL
Censor Librorum
March 25, 2008

Imprimatur: † Most Rev. Bernard J. Harrington, DD
Bishop of Winona
March 25, 2008

The publishing team for this book included Roxane Kadrlik Chlachula, Brian Singer-Towns, and John Vitek, editors; Lorraine Kilmartin, reviewer; Getty Images, cover photo; prepress and manufacturing coordinated by the production departments of Saint Mary's Press.

Printed in the United States of America

3461

ISBN 978-0-88489-738-5, Print
ISBN 978-1-59982-200-6, Digital

Library of Congress Cataloging-in-Publication Data

Singer-Towns, Brian.
   Catholic quick view : beliefs, definitions, prayers, practices, saints, and symbols / written by Brian Singer-Towns, Marilyn Kielbasa, and Robert Feduccia, Jr. — 2nd ed.
   p. cm.
ISBN 978-0-88489-738-5 (pbk.)
   1. Catholic Church—Doctrines. 2. Theology, Doctrinal—Popular works. 3. Catholic Church—Customs and practices. I. Kielbasa, Marilyn. II. Feduccia, Robert. III. Title.
BX1754.S575 2008
282—dc22

                                                                2008015630

Contents

Being Catholic: A Quick View

There are an estimated one billion Catholics living in the world. That is about 16 percent of the world's population. There are more Catholics than there are people in any other Christian denomination. There are also more Catholics than there are Jews, Hindus, or Buddhists—only Muslims have more members. The great number of Catholics in the world testifies to Catholicism's universal appeal and to the power the Catholic faith has in people's lives.

This book begins with a brief summary of key Catholic beliefs, practices, and attitudes. The book then introduces core Catholic spiritual beliefs, prayers, and liturgies, as well as Catholic signs and symbols and patron saints. A glossary of Catholic terms offers specific definitions of key Catholic beliefs and practices.

This book provides only a quick view of Catholic beliefs, practices, and attitudes. It does not offer an in-depth explanation as to why Catholics believe or practice what they do. For an in-depth exploration of the Catholic faith, you may wish to purchase *The Catholic Faith Handbook for Youth, Revised*, by Brian Singer-Towns (Winona, MN: Saint Mary's Press, 2008), from which the content of this book has been adapted.

Core Catholic Beliefs

- God created human beings to be in perfect union with God and one another. However, the sin of our first parents—called Original Sin—deprived the human race of our original holiness and justice.
- Throughout human history God worked to restore the relationship of love and trust that was lost through Original Sin. He did this by entering into covenants—special relationships based on mutual promises—with Noah, Abraham and Sarah, and the people of Israel. But the people often broke their covenant promises.
- Ultimately God sent his only begotten son, Jesus Christ, as savior for the human race. Christ was both fully God and fully man. He became the perfect sacrifice for the forgiveness of

sins and the restoration of the relationship of love and trust between God and humankind.

- Following his death Jesus was brought back to life in the Resurrection! Christ overcame death and opened Heaven's gates for all the just.
- The Holy Spirit has been at work in the world from the beginning of creation to the present day. The Holy Spirit is one with the Father and the Son, and is also called the Advocate (Paraclete) and the Spirit of Truth.
- God has revealed himself to be Trinity, that is, the mystery of one God in three divine Persons: Father, Son, and Holy Spirit. This mystery cannot be arrived at by reason but was revealed by Jesus Christ.
- Christ established the Catholic Church on the foundation of the Apostles. Christ and the Holy Spirit revealed the fullness of religious truth to the Apostles. The fullness of God's revealed truth is called Sacred Tradition and is entrusted to the Apostles' successors, the bishops of the Church.
- The Bible, or the Sacred Scriptures, is another source of God's revealed truth for Catholics. The Bible is closely connected to Sacred Tradition. The Holy Spirit inspired the authors of the Bible to write what God wants us to know for our salvation.
- All people are destined for eternal life after death. The baptized who have put their faith in Jesus Christ as their savior will find their eternal reward in heaven. Salvation through Christ is also possible for those who seek God with a sincere heart and try to do his will but who do not know Christ, the Gospel, or the Church through no fault of their own. Those who willfully and persistently reject God in this life will find their eternal punishment in hell.

Core Catholic Practices

- Catholics celebrate Seven Sacraments that form the basis of their worship, or communal prayer, together. The Seven Sacraments were instituted by Christ and entrusted to the Church to make the love of God real and present in the world.

- The Sacrament of the Eucharist is the heart of the Catholic Church's life. In the Sacrament, Catholics literally receive the Body and Blood of Christ in the appearance of bread and wine.
- Sunday, or the "Lord's Day," is the principal day for the celebration of the Eucharist. Catholics keep the day holy by attending Mass and resting from work, in honor of Christ's Resurrection.
- Catholics follow a special calendar with all the feasts and holy days of the liturgical year. The special seasons of Advent and Lent prepare them to understand God's great love, which is celebrated at Christmas and Easter.
- Catholics place a strong emphasis on living morally, because they believe they are called to new life in the Holy Spirit. The moral code for this new life is based on the Ten Commandments and the Beatitudes.
- Catholics defend the dignity of human life, and Catholic morality is often described as pro-life. Catholics are opposed to anything that threatens the sanctity of human life, including abortion, euthanasia, capital punishment, and human cloning.
- Serving people in need and working to transform society are essential elements of Catholic life. The Church is called to be a sign of God's perfect Kingdom yet to come, by working for justice and human rights in this life.
- Catholics honor the great people of faith who have preceded them, the saints, and in a dear and special way, Mary, the mother of Jesus.

Core Catholic Attitudes

- Catholics recognize that God is present to, in, and through all creation—including the natural world, persons, communities, and historical events. For Catholics all creation is sacred and has the potential to be a source of God's grace.
- Catholics place their trust in the essential goodness of the human person, who is made in the image of God, even though we are flawed by the effect of Original Sin.

- Catholics appreciate both faith and reason, both religion and science. Reason can lead to faith.
- Although the fullness of truth resides in the Catholic Church, Catholics seek to recognize and affirm the aspects of God's revealed truth that are shared with other religions and all people of good will.
- Because the human person is saved by participating in the community of faith—that is, the Church—rather than as isolated individuals, Catholics emphasize community life and communal worship. Catholics distrust any spirituality that reflects a primary attitude of "it's just God and me; I don't need a Church."
- Catholicism respects the great diversity of cultures in the world and is committed to proclaiming the message of Jesus to all people in all cultures at all times.
- Catholics respect and embrace a wide variety of spiritualities and prayer forms.

Core Catholic Teachings on Reason and Revelation

The Catholic Church makes frequent appeal to human reason in teaching about the religious truths God has revealed. The Church teaches:

- Revelation is God making himself and his Divine Plan known to the human race through words and deeds in human history.
- The human person must trust that God has revealed to the Church what he wants it to know for its salvation.
- In listening to the message of creation and the voice of conscience, every person can come to certainty about the existence of God.
- Through the natural light of human reason, the one true God can be known from his works—that is, from the world and from the human person. This is one reason why the Church teaches that salvation is possible for every person, even those who have never heard of Jesus Christ.

- God has revealed himself in order to restore the communion that human beings were created to have with him, before the relationship was broken by Original Sin.
- Revelation is communicated in the Bible's stories of how God made himself known to the Chosen People by acting throughout their history. But when those attempts met with failure, God took a radical step, sending his son, Jesus Christ, into the world as the savior. While remaining fully God, Jesus Christ took on a human nature; he is both true God and true man. Thus Jesus Christ is the fullest and complete Revelation of who God is, and through Christ, God established his covenant with the human race forever. As the Bible tells us, "[Christ] is the image of the invisible God" (Colossians 1:15).
- Everything needed to be known about God, everything needed to be known for eternal union with him, has been revealed in Christ. Nothing more needs to be added or taken away.

Core Catholic Teachings on the Scriptures and Tradition

The Catholic Church teaches:
- Christ promised to send the Holy Spirit to his closest followers, the Apostles, after he physically left them to ascend into Heaven: "When the Spirit of truth comes, he will guide you into all the truth" (John 16:13). The Holy Spirit helped the Apostles remember and understand all that Jesus did and taught. These truths about Jesus and his teaching are therefore called the Apostolic Tradition, or sometimes just the Tradition.
- Under the inspiration of the Holy Spirit, the Apostles handed on everything they knew about Jesus to the first Christians and to the generation of leaders who followed them.
- The Holy Spirit inspired people in the early Church to create written documents explaining what the Apostles had handed down about Jesus.
- The Scriptures and Tradition are two sources of Revelation. They are closely connected, and together form a single sacred deposit of truth under the guidance of the Holy Spirit. They

can never be in conflict, and each one helps us to understand the other.

- The Church looks to God's Revelation in the Scriptures and Tradition as the only authentic and complete source for knowledge about God and God's will for the whole human race. It is the responsibility of the Church, through its teaching, worship, and ministries, to transmit to every new generation all that God has revealed.
- As the successors of the Apostles, it is the particular and exclusive responsibility of the bishops in union with the Pope—who are also called the Magisterium—to faithfully teach, interpret, and preserve the Scriptures and Tradition for all believers until Christ returns in glory.

The Organization of the Catholic Bible

The books of the Bible are actually organized into sections. The Old Testament has forty-six books divided into the following sections:

- **The Pentateuch (Genesis through Deuteronomy).** These five books are the core of the Old Testament. They tell the stories of Creation, sin, and the origin of God's Chosen People.
- **The Historical Books (Joshua through 2 Maccabees).** These books tell how the Israelites settled in the Promised Land. They also tell the stories of their great—and not-so-great—kings.
- **The Wisdom Books (Job through Sirach).** These are books of poetry and the collected wisdom of the Israelites.
- **The Prophets (Isaiah through Malachi).** These books are the collected speeches and biographies of the Israelite prophets. The prophets spoke for God against idolatry and injustice.

The New Testament has twenty-seven books divided into the following sections:

- **The Gospels (Matthew, Mark, Luke, and John).** These four books are the most important books for Christians because they convey the meaning of Christ Jesus' life and teaching as their central message.

- **The Acts of the Apostles.** This book is a continuation of the Gospel of Luke and tells the stories of how the early Church was spread.
- **The Epistles (Romans through Jude).** These are twenty-one letters, written by Paul and other early Church leaders, that give teachings and guidance to individuals and the first Christian churches.
- **The Book of Revelation.** This book records the visions of an early Christian named John.

Core Catholic Understandings on Biblical Inspiration and Interpretation

The way Catholics interpret the Bible has been a source of conflict between Catholics and some other Christians.

- All Christians believe that God is the ultimate author of the Bible because the Holy Spirit inspired the human authors in their writing. But some Christians—sometimes called fundamentalists or literalists—believe that every part of the Bible must be absolutely true in every way: historically true, geographically true, and scientifically true. Thus, for example, they believe that God created the world in six twenty-four-hour days.
- The Catholic Church teaches that the Holy Spirit inspired the biblical authors to write what God wanted known for salvation. The Holy Spirit did not take over the biblical authors' humanity when they wrote. Thus the authors were subject to natural human limitations, and they also used their human creativity in their writing. To continue the earlier example, Catholics believe in the religious truth that God created the world and everything in it, without having to believe that the world was literally created in six twenty-four-hour days.
- Catholics understand that the Bible is without error in communicating what God wants known for salvation without having to be historically and scientifically correct in every detail.

Core Catholic Spirituality, Prayers, and Liturgies

Two Great Commandments

- You shall love the Lord your God with all your heart, with all your soul, and all your mind, and with all your strength.
- You shall love your neighbor as yourself.

(Matthew 22:37–40, Mark 12:29–31, Luke 10:27)

Ten Commandments

1. I am the Lord your God: you shall not have strange gods before me.
2. You shall not take the name of the Lord, your God, in vain.
3. Remember to keep holy the Lord's Day.
4. Honor your father and mother.
5. You shall not kill.
6. You shall not commit adultery.
7. You shall not steal.
8. You shall not bear false witness against your neighbor.
9. You shall not covet your neighbor's wife.
10. You shall not covet your neighbor's goods.

Beatitudes

- Blessed are the poor in spirit, the kingdom of heaven is theirs.
- Blessed are they who mourn, they will be comforted.
- Blessed are the meek, they will inherit the earth.
- Blessed are they who hunger and thirst for righteousness, they will be satisfied.
- Blessed are the merciful, they will be shown mercy.
- Blessed are the clean of heart, they will see God.
- Blessed are the peacemakers, they will be called children of God.
- Blessed are they who are persecuted for the sake of righteousness, the kingdom of heaven is theirs.

Corporal Works of Mercy

- Feed the hungry.
- Give drink to the thirsty.
- Shelter the homeless.
- Clothe the naked.
- Care for the sick.
- Help the imprisoned.
- Bury the dead.

Spiritual Works of Mercy

- Share knowledge.
- Give advice to those who need it.
- Comfort those who suffer.
- Be patient with others.
- Forgive those who hurt you.
- Give correction to those who need it.
- Pray for the living and the dead.

Theological Virtues

- Faith
- Hope
- Love

Cardinal Virtues

- Prudence
- Justice
- Fortitude
- Temperance

Seven Gifts of the Holy Spirit

- **Wisdom.** Through wisdom, the wonders of nature, every event in history, and all the ups and downs of our lives take on deeper meaning and purpose. The wise person sees where the Spirit of God is at work and is able to share that insight with others. Wisdom is the fullest expression of the gifts of knowledge and understanding.
- **Understanding.** The gift of understanding is the ability to comprehend how a person must live her or his life as a follower of Jesus. Through the gift of understanding, Christians realize that the Gospel tells them not just who Jesus is but also who we are. The gift of understanding is closely related to the gifts of knowledge and wisdom.
- **Right judgment.** The gift of right judgment is the ability to know the difference between right and wrong and then to choose what is good. It helps us to act on and live out what Jesus has taught. In the exercise of right judgment, many of the other gifts—especially understanding, wisdom, and often courage—come into play in the Christian's daily life.
- **Courage.** The gift of courage enables us to take risks and to overcome fear as we try to live out the Gospel of Jesus. Followers of Jesus confront many challenges and even danger—the risk of being laughed at, the fear of rejection, and, for some believers, the fear of physical harm and even death. The Spirit gives Christians the strength to confront and ultimately overcome such challenges.
- **Knowledge.** The gift of knowledge is the ability to comprehend the basic meaning and message of Jesus. Jesus revealed the will of God, his Father, and taught people what they need to know to achieve fullness of life and, ultimately, salvation. The gift of knowledge is closely related to the gifts of understanding and wisdom.
- **Reverence.** Sometimes called piety, the gift of reverence gives the Christian a deep sense of respect for God. Jesus spoke of his Father, God, as "Abba," a very intimate name similar to "Daddy" or "Pappa." Through the gift of reverence, we can come before God with the openness and trust of small children, totally dependent on the One who created us.

- **Wonder and awe.** The gift of wonder and awe in the presence of God is sometimes translated as "the fear of the Lord." Though we can approach God with the trust of little children, we are also often aware of God's total majesty, unlimited power, and desire for justice. A child may want to sit on the lap of his loving Father, but sometimes the believer will fall on her knees in the presence of the Creator of the universe.

Fruits of the Holy Spirit

- Charity
- Joy
- Peace
- Patience
- Goodness
- Kindness
- Long suffering
- Humility
- Faithfulness
- Modesty
- Continence
- Chastity

Four Marks of the Catholic Church

- One
- Holy
- Catholic
- Apostolic

Liturgical Year

- Advent
- Christmas
- Ordinary Time
- Lent
- Easter Triduum
- Easter
- Pentecost
- Ordinary Time

Seven Sacraments

- Baptism
- Confirmation
- The Eucharist
- Penance and Reconciliation
- Anointing of the Sick
- Matrimony
- Holy Orders

Precepts of the Church

1. To keep holy the day of the Lord's Resurrection; to worship God by participating in Mass every Sunday and on the holy days of obligation; to avoid those activities that would hinder renewal of the soul and body on the Sabbath (for example, needless work or unnecessary shopping).
2. To lead a sacramental life; to receive Holy Communion frequently and the Sacrament of Penance and Reconciliation regularly—minimally, to receive the Sacrament of Penance and Reconciliation at least once a year (annual confession is obligatory only if serious sin is involved); minimally also, to receive Holy Communion at least once a year between the first Sunday of Lent and Trinity Sunday.
3. To study Catholic teaching in preparation for the Sacrament of Confirmation, to be confirmed, and then to continue to study and advance the cause of Christ.
4. To observe the marriage laws of the Church; to give religious training, by example and word, to one's children; to use parish schools and catechetical programs.
5. To strengthen and support the Church—one's own parish community and parish priests, the worldwide Church, and the Pope.
6. To do penance, including abstaining from meat and fasting from food on the appointed days.
7. To join in the missionary spirit and apostolate (work) of the Church.

Holy Days of Obligation

- Christmas (December 25)
- Solemnity of the Blessed Virgin Mary, the Mother of God (January 1)
- Ascension of the Lord (the Sunday that follows forty days after Easter)
- Assumption of the Blessed Virgin Mary (August 15)
- All Saints (November 1)
- Immaculate Conception of the Blessed Virgin Mary (December 8)

Regulations on Fasting and Abstinence

The Catholic Church requires its members to observe certain dietary rules—fasting and abstinence—in order to recognize and mark the importance of particular days during its liturgical year, as well as to express penance for personal sin. The regulations apply as follows:

- Generally, the laws of fasting require that on the designated days the person eat just one full meal, two smaller meals, and avoid eating between meals. Abstinence laws require that the person avoid meat altogether.
- The regulations governing abstinence from meat apply to all Catholics age fourteen and older. From the completion of their eighteenth year until the beginning of their sixtieth year, adults are bound by the regulations that govern fasting. Pregnant women and sick people are excused from the regulations.
- Ash Wednesday and Good Friday are days of both fasting and abstinence; all the other Fridays of Lent are days of abstinence only.
- In addition, the Church encourages its adult members to observe some form of penance, perhaps including some kind of fast and abstinence, on all Fridays throughout the year.
- The Church also calls for fasting prior to receiving Communion during the Mass. In this case the fast helps prepare the mind and heart for the great gift of the Eucharist by doing something physical to help focus attention. Church law calls for Catholics to avoid all food and drink, with the exception of water and medicine, for one hour before receiving

Communion. This regulation does not apply to sick people or others for whom such restrictions would jeopardize health.

Parts of the Mass

Introductory Rites
- Entrance Chant
- Greeting
- Penitential Act
- *Kyrie*
- Gloria
- Opening Prayer (Collect)

Liturgy of the Word
- First Reading
- Responsorial Psalm
- Second Reading
- Gospel Acclamation
- Gospel Reading
- Homily
- Profession of Faith (Nicene Creed or Apostles' Creed)
- Prayer of the Faithful

Liturgy of the Eucharist
- Presentation and Preparation of the Gifts
- Prayer over the Offerings
- Eucharistic Prayer   Preface
  Holy, Holy, Holy
  Memorial Acclamation
  Concluding Doxology
- Communion Rite: The Lord's Prayer
  Sign of Peace
  Lamb of God
  Communion
  Prayer after Communion

Concluding Rites
- Final Blessing
- Dismissal

Catholic Prayers and Devotions

Act of Contrition

My God, I am sorry for my sins
with all my heart, and I detest them.
In choosing to do wrong and failing to do good,
I have sinned against you,
whom I should love above all things.
I firmly intend, with your help,
to do penance, to sin no more,
and to avoid whatever leads me to sin.
Our savior Jesus Christ suffered and died for us.
In his name, my God, have mercy.

Act of Faith

My God, I firmly believe you are one God in three Divine Persons,
    Father, Son, and Holy Spirit.
I believe in Jesus Christ, your son, who became man and died for
    our sins, and who will come to judge the living and the dead.
I believe these and all the truths which the Holy Catholic Church
    teaches, because you have revealed them, who can neither
    deceive nor be deceived.
Amen.

Act of Hope

O my God, trusting in your infinite goodness and promises, I
hope to obtain pardon of my sins, the help of your grace, and
life everlasting, through the merits of Jesus Christ, my Lord and
redeemer. Amen.

Act of Love

My God, I love you above all things, with my whole heart and
soul, because you are all-good and worthy of all my love. I love
my neighbor as myself for love of you. I forgive all who have
injured me, and I ask pardon of all whom I have injured. Amen.

Angelus

The angel of the Lord declared unto Mary,
And she conceived of the Holy Spirit.
   Hail Mary . . .
Behold the handmaid of the Lord,
Be it done unto me according to your word.
   Hail Mary . . .
And the Word was made flesh,
And dwelt among us.
   Hail Mary . . .
Pray for us, O Holy Mother of God, that we may be made worthy
of the promises of Christ. Let us pray: Pour forth, we beseech
you, O Lord, your grace into our hearts that we to whom the
incarnation of Christ, your Son, was made known by the mes-
sage of an angel may, by his passion and cross, be brought to the
glory of his resurrection, through Christ our Lord.

Apostles' Creed

I believe in God, the Father almighty, Creator of heaven and earth,
and in Jesus Christ, his only Son, our Lord, who was conceived by
the Holy Spirit, born of the Virgin Mary, suffered under Pontius
Pilate, was crucified, died and was buried; he descended into
hell; on the third day he rose again from the dead; he ascended
into heaven, and is seated at the right hand of God the Father
almighty; from there he will come to judge the living and the dead.

   I believe in the Holy Spirit, the holy catholic Church, the communion of saints, the forgiveness of sins, the resurrection of the
body, and life everlasting. Amen.

Confiteor (I Confess)

I confess to almighty God and to you, my brothers and sisters,
that I have greatly sinned in my thoughts and in my words, in
what I have done and in what I have failed to do, through my
fault, through my fault, through my most grievous fault; therefore
I ask blessed Mary ever-Virgin, all the Angels and Saints, and you,
my brothers and sisters, to pray for me to the Lord our God.

Glory Be

Glory be to the Father, and to the Son, and to the Holy Spirit, as it was in the beginning, is now, and will be forever. Amen.

Grace Before Meals

Bless us, O Lord, and these your gifts,
which we are about to receive
from your bounty,
through Christ our Lord. Amen.

Grace After Meals

We give you thanks, almighty God,
for these and all your gifts
which we have received
through Christ our Lord. Amen.

Hail Mary

Hail Mary, full of grace,
the Lord is with you;
blessed are you among women,
and blessed is the fruit of your womb, Jesus.

Holy Mary, Mother of God,
pray for us sinners
now and at the hour of our death.
Amen.

Lord's Prayer (also called the Our Father)

Our Father who art in heaven,
hallowed be thy name.
Thy kingdom come.
Thy will be done on earth, as it is in heaven.
Give us this day our daily bread,
and forgive us our trespasses,
as we forgive those who trespass against us,
and lead us not into temptation,
but deliver us from evil. Amen.

Magnificat (Mary's Song) (cf. Luke 1:46–55)

My being proclaims the greatness of the Lord,
my spirit finds joy in God my savior.
For he has looked upon his servant
in all her lowliness.
All ages to come shall call me blessed.
God who is mighty
has done great things for me, holy is his name;
his mercy is from age to age
on those who fear him.
He has shown might with his arm;
he has confused the proud
in their inmost thoughts.
He has deposed the mighty from their thrones
and raised the lowly to high places.

The hungry he has given every good thing
while the rich he has sent empty away.
He has upheld Israel his servant,
ever mindful of his mercy,
even as he promised our fathers,
promised Abraham and his descendants
forever.

Memorare

Remember, O most gracious Virgin Mary, that never was it
known that anyone who fled to your protection, implored your
help, or sought your intercession was left unaided. Inspired by
this confidence, we fly unto you, O virgin of virgins, our mother.
To you do we come, before you we stand, sinful and sorrowful.
O mother of the Word Incarnate, despise not our petitions, but in
your mercy, hear and answer us.

Morning Prayer

Almighty God, I thank you for your past blessings. Today I
offer myself—whatever I do, say, or think—to your loving care.
Continue to bless me, Lord. I make this morning offering in union

with the divine intentions of Jesus Christ who offers himself
daily in the holy sacrifice of the Mass, and in union with Mary,
his Virgin Mother and our Mother, who was always the faithful
handmaid of the Lord. Amen.

Nicene Creed

I believe in one God,
the Father almighty,
maker of heaven and earth,
of all things visible and invisible.

I believe in one Lord Jesus Christ,
the Only Begotten Son of God,
born of the Father before all ages.
God from God, Light from Light,
true God from true God,
begotten, not made, consubstantial with the Father;
through him all things were made.
For us men and for our salvation
he came down from heaven,
and by the Holy Spirit was incarnate of the Virgin Mary,
and became man.

For our sake he was crucified under Pontius Pilate,
he suffered death and was buried,
and rose again on the third day
in accordance with the Scriptures.
He ascended into heaven
and is seated at the right hand of the Father.
He will come again in glory
to judge the living and the dead
and his kingdom will have no end.

I believe in the Holy Spirit, the Lord, the giver of life,
who proceeds from the Father and the Son,
who with the Father and the Son is adored and glorified,
who has spoken through the prophets.

I believe in one, holy, catholic and apostolic Church.
I confess one baptism for the forgiveness of sins
and I look forward to the resurrection of the dead
and the life of the world to come. Amen.

"Prayer of Saint Francis"

Lord, make me an instrument of your peace:
>   where there is hatred, let me sow love;
>   where there is injury, pardon;
>   where there is doubt, faith;
>   where there is despair, hope;
>   where there is darkness, light;
>   where there is sadness, joy.

Divine Master,
>   grant that I may not so much seek
>   to be consoled as to console,
>   to be understood as to understand,
>   to be loved as to love.

For it is in giving that we receive,
>   it is in pardoning that we are pardoned,
>   it is in dying that we are born to eternal life.

"Prayer to the Holy Spirit"

Come, Holy Spirit, fill the hearts of your faithful. Enkindle in them the fire of your love. Send forth your Spirit, and they will be created. And you will renew the face of the earth.

Let us pray:

Lord, by the light of the Holy Spirit, you have taught the hearts of the faithful. In the same Spirit, help us to relish what is right and always rejoice in your consolation. We ask this through Christ our Lord. Amen.

The Rosary

The rosary is perhaps the most popular devotion to Mary, the Mother of God. The central part of the rosary consists of the recitation of five sets of ten Hail Marys (each set is called a decade). Each new decade begins by saying an Our Father, and each decade concludes with a Glory Be. The pray-er keeps track of the prayers said by moving from one bead to the next in order.

The recitation of the rosary begins with a series of prayers, said in the following order while using as a guide a small chain of beads and a crucifix:

1. the sign of the cross
2. the Apostles' Creed
3. one Our Father
4. three Hail Marys
5. one Glory Be

After these introductory prayers, the recitation of the decades, as described above, begins.

The saying of a five-decade rosary is connected with meditation on what are called the mysteries of the life of Jesus. These mysteries too are collected into series of five—five joyful, five sorrowful, five glorious, and five luminous mysteries (recently added by Pope John Paul II). The mysteries of the rosary are listed below. The pray-er devotes one recitation of the rosary to each set of mysteries. He or she chooses which set of mysteries to meditate on while saying the decades of Hail Marys. Therefore, the complete rosary consists of twenty decades.

With a little practice, regular praying of the rosary can become a source of great inspiration and consolation for the Christian.

Joyful Mysteries

- The Annunciation
- The Visitation
- The Birth of Our Lord
- The Presentation of Jesus in the Temple
- The Finding of Jesus in the Temple

Sorrowful Mysteries

- The Agony of Jesus in the Garden
- The Scourging at the Pillar
- The Crowning of Thorns
- The Carrying of the Cross
- The Crucifixion

Glorious Mysteries

- The Resurrection of Jesus
- The Ascension of Jesus into Heaven
- The Descent of the Holy Spirit on the Apostles (Pentecost)
- The Assumption of Mary into Heaven
- The Crowning of Mary as Queen of Heaven

Luminous Mysteries

- The Baptism of Jesus
- Jesus Reveals Himself in the Miracle at Cana
- Jesus Proclaims the Good News of the Kingdom of God
- The Transfiguration of Jesus
- The Institution of the Eucharist

Sign of the Cross

In the name of the Father, and of the Son, and of the Holy Spirit. Amen.

Stations of the Cross

1. Jesus is condemned to death.
2. Jesus takes up his cross.
3. Jesus falls the first time.
4. Jesus meets his mother.
5. Simon helps Jesus carry the cross.
6. Veronica wipes the face of Jesus.
7. Jesus falls the second time.
8. Jesus meets the women of Jerusalem.
9. Jesus falls the third time.
10. Jesus is stripped of his garments.
11. Jesus is nailed to the cross.
12. Jesus dies on the cross.
13. Jesus is taken down from the cross.
14. Jesus is laid in the tomb.

Catholic Signs and Symbols

 **Alpha and Omega.** The first and last letters of the Greek alphabet. They appear together on the Paschal candle and signify the eternal presence of Jesus Christ. He is the beginning and the end.

 **Altar.** The central focal point in a church and a symbol of Christ. It is the place where the sacrifice of the cross is made present and truly re-encountered. It is also the table of the Lord to which the People of God are called to celebrate Mass.

 **Ambo.** The lectern from which the Word of God is proclaimed.

 **Ashes.** From burnt palms, ashes remind us of our sins and our need for God.

Baptismal Pool. A large tank of water used for Baptism by immersion. Being baptized unites one with the Paschal mystery of Jesus Christ—his life, suffering, death, Resurrection, and Ascension—and with the entire Church.

Bread. Bread symbolizes the goodness of God's creation and the work of our lives. It is both God's gift to us and our gift to God, because we give that which we have already received from God. Through Consecration and the action of the Holy Spirit, it becomes the Body of Christ.

Candle, Altar. The candles placed near the altar and always lit during Mass to signify that Christ is the light.

Candle, Paschal. The large white candle that is lit at the Easter Vigil. It is a symbol of the Resurrection of Jesus Christ, who dispels the darkness of death.

Chalice. The cup used during Mass that holds the wine before the Consecration and the Blood of Christ after the Consecration. It is a symbol of Jesus' sacrifice and eternal life. Before Jesus died he prayed: "Father, if you are willing, remove this cup from me; yet, not my will but yours be done" (Luke 22:42).

Chi Rho. An ancient symbol for Christ. X (chi) and P (rho) are the first two letters in the Greek word for "Christ."

Chrism. Olive oil mixed with fragrant balsam and consecrated by the bishop. A sign of the gift of the Holy Spirit, it is used for Baptism, Confirmation, Holy Orders, and the dedication of churches and altars.

Crosier. A staff that resembles a shepherd's crook carried by bishops to signify their pastoral and authoritative role in the Church.

Crucifix. A cross with a representation of Jesus' dead body. It is a symbol of paradox: new life comes though death.

Dove. A symbol of the Holy Spirit. All four Gospels describe the Holy Spirit's coming upon Jesus in the form of a dove.

Holy Water Font. A small receptacle for blessed water found at church entrances. Making the sign of the cross with water from the font when we gather for liturgy reminds us of Baptism and calls us to recommit ourselves to the Gospel and turn away from sin.

Ichthus. This word is Greek for "fish." Early Christians used the term to refer to "Jesus Christ, God's Son, Savior" *(Iesous Christus, Theou Uios, Soter)*. In Greek the first letter of each word in the phrase spells the word for "fish."

IHS. The first three letters of Jesus' name in Greek: *iota* (I), *eta* (H), *sigma* (S).

Incense. The fragrant smoke rising from burning incense is a symbol of prayers rising up to God.

INRI. An abbreviation of the Latin phrase, *Iesus Nazarenus Rex Iudaeorum.* The Gospel of John (19:19) says Pilate had this written in three languages and put on Jesus' cross. It means "Jesus of Nazareth, King of the Jews."

Lily. A symbol of the Resurrection of Jesus Christ. The lily is a beautiful flower that springs forth from a seemingly dead bulb.

Miter. The tall, pointed hat worn by the bishop during liturgical celebrations to symbolize his authority.

Oil of Catechumens. Olive oil blessed for use in pre-baptismal anointings. During the period of preparation for Baptism, catechumens are anointed. This signifies cleansing and strengthening.

Oil of the Sick. Olive oil blessed for use in the Sacrament of the Anointing of the Sick. The anointing of the seriously ill and those who are near death expresses comfort and healing.

Palm. A symbol of triumph. In John's Gospel Jesus was hailed as king by people waving palm branches in celebration as he entered Jerusalem. This is remembered on Palm Sunday.

People. The assembly of people gathered for Mass is a visible expression of the Church. Christ is present during the Eucharistic Liturgy in many ways. Among those ways is when the faithful people gather in prayer and song.

Sacred Minister. A term for the ordained minister who presides at Mass. The sacred minister acts as the person Christ, and Christ is present in him.

Sanctuary Lamp. The light that burns near the tabernacle to indicate the presence of the Blessed Sacrament. The light serves as a reminder that Christ, the light, is with us.

Tabernacle. A safe, secure cabinet where the consecrated bread, or Blessed Sacrament, is kept. The Body of Christ is reserved so it can be distributed to the sick and dying. The tabernacle fosters adoration of the Blessed Sacrament by the faithful.

Triqueta. This interlocking symbol is an early Christian symbol of the Blessed Trinity. Its interwoven arcs of equal length signify the equality of the three Persons of the Trinity—Father, Son, and Holy Spirit. The continuity of the form recalls the unity in the Trinity.

Water. A symbol of both life and death. It cleanses and refreshes and is necessary for life. It can also lead to destruction and death by drowning. Water is a central symbol for Christians because in Baptism it signifies that we die with Christ and rise to new life with him.

White Garment. After Baptism newly initiated Catholics are clothed in white garments to signify they are new creations in Christ Jesus.

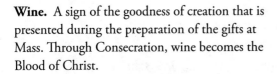

Wine. A sign of the goodness of creation that is presented during the preparation of the gifts at Mass. Through Consecration, wine becomes the Blood of Christ.

Word. Jesus is the Word of God who became man. "The Word became flesh and lived among us" (John 1:14). At the Eucharistic Liturgy, when the Word of God is proclaimed, Christ is present and speaks to the gathered faithful.

Patron Saints and Their Causes

A

Accountants, Saint Matthew, *September 21*
Actors, Saint Genesius, *August 25*
Addicts, Saint Maximilian Maria Kolbe, *August 14*
Advertising, Saint Bernardino of Siena, *May 20*
AIDS patients, Saint Peregrine Laziosi, *May 16*
Air travelers, Saint Joseph of Cupertino, *September 18*
Alcoholics, Venerable Matt Talbot, Saint Monica, *August 27*
Altar servers, Saint John Berchmans, *November 26*
Animals, Saint Francis of Assisi, *October 4*
Archaeologists, Saint Helen, *August 18*
Architects, Saint Thomas the Apostle, *July 3*
Art, Saint Catherine of Bologna, *May 9*
Artists, Saint Luke, *October 18;* Saint Catherine of Bologna, *May 9;* Blessed Fra Angelico, *February 18*
Astronauts, Saint Joseph of Cupertino, *September 18*
Astronomers, Saint Dominic, *August 8*
Athletes, Saint Sebastian, *January 20*
Attorneys, Saint Thomas More, *June 22;* Saint Raymond of Penyafort, *January 7*
Authors, Saint Francis de Sales, *January 24*

B

Babies, Saint Nicholas of Tolentino, *September 10*
Bakers, Saint Elizabeth of Hungary, *November 17;* Saint Nicholas of Myra, *December 6*

Bankers, Saint Matthew, *September 21*

Baptism, Saint John the Baptist, *June 24*

Barbers, Saints Cosmas and Damian, *September 26;* Saint Martin de Porres, *November 3*

Beggars, Saint Alexis, *July 17;* Saint Giles, *September 1*

Blindness, Raphael (Michael, Gabriel, and Raphael), *September 29;* Saint Lucy, *December 13*

Bodily ills, Our Lady of Lourdes, *February 11*

Bookkeepers, Saint Matthew, *September 21*

Booksellers, Saint John of God, *March 8*

Boys, Saint John Bosco, *January 31*

Breast disease, against, Saint Agatha, *February 5*

Brides, Saint Nicholas of Myra, *December 6*

Broadcasters, Saint Gabriel, *September 29*

Builders, Saint Barbara, *December 4;* Saint Vincent Ferrer, *April 5*

Businessmen, Saint Homobonus, *November 13*

Businesswomen, Saint Margaret Clitherow, *March 26*

C

Cab drivers, Saint Fiacre, *August 30*

Cancer patients, Saint Peregrine Laziosi, *May 16*

Carpenters, Saint Joseph, *March 19*

Catechists, Saint Charles Borromeo, *November 4;* Saint Robert Bellarmine, *September 17;* Saint Viator, *December 14*

Catechumens, Saint Charles Borromeo, *November 4;* Saint Robert Bellarmine, *September 17*

Catholic schools, Saint Thomas Aquinas, *January 28*

Catholic youth, Saint Aloysius Gonzaga, *June 21;* Saint Maria Goretti, *July 6*

Charities, Saint Vincent de Paul, *September 27*

Childbirth, Saint Gerard Majella, *October 16;* Saint Raymond Nonnatus, *August 31*

Children, Saint Nicholas, *December 6*

Church, Saint Joseph, *March 19*

Civil servants, Saint Thomas More, *June 22*

Clergy, Saint Gabriel of Our Lady of Sorrows, *September 15*

Colleges, Saint Thomas Aquinas, *January 28*

Comedians, Saint Vitus, *June 15*

Communication workers, Saint Gabriel, *September 29*

Computers, Saint Isidore of Seville, *April 4*

Construction workers, Saint Thomas the Apostle, *July 3*

Cooks, Saint Thomas the Apostle, *July 3;* Saint Lawrence, *August 10*

Court clerks, Saint Thomas More, *June 22*

D

Dairy workers, Saint Brigid of Kildare, *February 1*

Dancers, Saint Vitus, *June 15*

Deacons, Saint Stephen, *December 26*

Deafness, Saint Francis de Sales, *January 24*

Death, Saint Joseph, *March 19;* Saint Michael, *September 29*

Dentists, Saint Apollonia, *February 9*

Desperate causes, Saint Jude, *October 28*

Difficult marriages, Saint Rita of Cascia, *May 22*

Disabilities, Saint Giles, *September 1*

Disasters, Saint Genevieve, *January 3*

Doctors, Saint Luke, *October 18*

Domestic workers, Saint Zita of Lucca, *April 27*

Drivers, Saint Fiacre, *August 30*

Drug addiction, Saint Maximilian Maria Kolbe, *August 14*

E

Earthquakes, Saint Francis Borgia, *October 10*

Ecology, Saint Francis of Assisi, *October 4*

Editors, Saint John Bosco, *January 31*

Engineers, Saint Patrick, *March 17;* Saint Ferdinand III, *May 30*

Epilepsy, Saint Dymphna, *May 30;* Saint Vitus, *June 15;* Saint
Willibrord, *November 7*

Eye disorders, Saint Clare, *August 11;* Saint Lucy, *December 13*

F

Falsely accused, Saint Raymond Nonnatus, *August 31*

Farmers, Saint Isidore the Farmer, *May 15*

Fathers, Saint Joseph, *March 19*

Firefighters, Saint Florian, *May 4;* Saint John of God, *March 8*

Fishermen, Saint Andrew, *November 30;* Saint Peter, *June 29*

Florists, Saint Thérèse of Lisieux, *October 1;* Saint Rose of Lima, *August 23;* Saint Dorothy, *February 6*

Funeral directors, Saint Joan of Arc, *May 30*

G

Gambling, compulsive, Saint Bernardine of Siena, *May 20*

Gardeners, Saint Adelard, *January 2;* Saint Fiacre, *August 30*

Girls, Saint Agnes, *January 21;* Saint Maria Goretti, *July 6*

Grandparents, Saints Ann and Joachim, *July 26*

Grocers, Saint Michael, *September 29*

Grooms, Saint Louis of France, *August 25;* Saint Nicholas, *December 6*

H

Hairdressers, Saint Martin de Porres, *November 3*

Headaches, Saint Teresa of Ávila, *October 15*

Heart patients, Saint John of God, *March 8*

Homeless, Saint Benedict, *July 11;* Joseph Labre, *April 17*

Hospital administrators, Saint Frances Xavier Cabrini, *November 13*

Hospitals, Saint Camillus de Lellis, *July 14;* Saint John of God, *March 8*

Hotel keepers, Saint Amand, *February 6*

Housewives, Saints Ann and Joachim, *July 26;* Saint Martha, *July 29*

Hunters, Saint Hubert, *November 3;* Saint Eustachius, *September 20*

I

Immigrants, Saint Frances Xavier Cabrini, *November 13*

Impossible causes, Saint Frances Xavier Cabrini, *November 13;* Saint Rita of Cascia, *May 22;* Saint Jude, *June 19*

Infertility, Saint Rita of Cascia, *May 22;* Saint Philomena, *August 11*
Insanity, Saint Dymphna, *May 30*
Internet, Saint Isidore of Seville, *April 4*
Invalids, Saint Roch, *August 16*

J

Jewelers, Saint Eligius, *December 1*
Journalists, Saint Francis de Sales, *January 24*
Judges, Saint John of Capistrano, *October 23*
Juvenile delinquents, Saint Dominic Savio, *March 9*

K

Kidney disease, Saint Benedict, *July 11*
Knee problems, Saint Roch, *August 16*

L

Laborers, Saint Isidore the Farmer, *May 15;* Saint James the Greater,
    July 25
Learning, Saint Ambrose, *December 7*
Librarians, Saint Jerome, *September 30*
Longevity, Saint Peter, *June 29*
Loss of parents, Saint Elizabeth Ann Seton, *January 24*
Lost items, Saint Anthony of Padua, *June 13*
Lovers, Saint Valentine, *February 14*

M

Married women, Saint Monica, *August 27*
Medical technicians, Saint Albert the Great, *November 15*
Mentally ill, Saint Dymphna, *May 30*
Merchants, Saint Francis of Assisi, *October 4;* Saint Nicholas,
    December 6
Messengers, Saint Gabriel, *September 29*
Midwives, Saint Raymond Nonnatus, *August 31*
Military members, Saint Joan of Arc, *May 30*
Miscarriage, prevention of, Saint Catherine of Sweden, *March 24*

Missionaries, Saint Francis Xavier, *December 3;* Saint Thérèse of Lisieux, *October 1*

Monks, Saint John the Baptist, *June 24*

Mothers, Saint Monica, *August 27*

Motorists, Saint Frances of Rome, *March 9*

Musicians, Saint Cecilia, *November 22*

Mystics, Saint John of the Cross, *December 14*

N

Neurological diseases, Saint Dymphna, *May 30*

Nuns, Saint Scholastica, *February 10;* Saint Brigid of Kildare, *February 1*

Nurses, Saint Camillus de Lellis, *July 14;* Saint John of God, *March 8;* Saint Agatha, *February 5*

O

Obstetricians, Saint Raymond Nonnatus, *August 31*

Orphans, abandoned children, Saint Jerome Emiliani, *February 8*

P

Painters, Saint Luke, *October 18*

Paralysis, Saint Osmund, *December 4*

Parenthood, Saint Rita of Cascia, *May 22*

Penitents, Saint Mary Magdalene, *July 22*

Pharmacists, Saints Cosmas and Damian, *September 26*

Philosophers, Saint Catherine of Alexandria, *November 25;* Saint Albert the Great, *November 15*

Physicians, Saint Luke, *October 18;* Saints Cosmas and Damian, *September 26*

Pilots, Saint Joseph of Cupertino, *September 18;* Saint Thérèse of Lisieux, *October 1*

Poets, Saint Columba, *June 9;* Saint David of Wales, *March 1*

Poisoning, Saint Benedict, *July 11*

Police officers, Saint Michael, *September 29*

Politicians, public servants, Saint Thomas More, *June 22*

Popes, Saint Peter, *June 29*

Postal workers, Saint Gabriel, *September 29*

Poverty, Saint Anthony of Padua, *June 13;* Saint Lawrence, *August 10*

Preachers, Saint John Chrysostom, *September 13*

Pregnant women, Saints Ann and Joachim, *July 26;* Saint Gerard Majella, *October 16;* Saint Margaret, *July 20;* Saint Raymond Nonnatus, *August 31*

Priests, Saint John Vianney, *August 4*

Printers, Saint Augustine, *August 28;* Saint John of God, *March 8*

Prisoners, Saint Dismas, *March 28;* Saint Joseph Cafasso, *June 23*

Public relations, Saint Bernardine of Siena, *May 20*

R

Race relations, Saint Martin de Porres, *November 3*

Radio, Saint Gabriel, *September 29*

Reconciliation, Saint Vincent Ferrer, *April 5*

Retreats, Saint Ignatius of Loyola, *July 31*

Rheumatism, Saint James the Greater, *July 25*

Robbers, danger from, Saint Leonard of Noblac, *November 6*

S

Sailors, Saint Elmo, *June 2;* Saint Brendan, *May 16;* Saint Francis of Paola, *April 2*

Savings, Saint Anthony Claret, *October 24*

Scholars, Saint Brigid of Kildare, *February 1;* Saint Bede the Venerable, *May 25*

Schools, Saint Thomas Aquinas, *January 28*

Scientists, Saint Albert the Great, *November 15*

Sculptors, Saint Claude, *February 15*

Secretaries, Saint Genesius, *August 25*

Seminarians, Saint Charles Borromeo, *November 4*

Servants, Saint Sava, *January 14;* Saint Zita of Lucca, *April 27*

Sickness, Saint John of God, *March 8*

Skin diseases, Saint Anthony the Abbot, *January 17*

Sobriety, Venerable Matt Talbot, *June 7*

Social justice, Saint Joseph, *March 19;* Saint Martin de Porres, *November 3*

Social workers, Saint Louise de Marillac, *March 15*

Soldiers, Saint George, *April 23;* Saint Martin of Tours, *November 11*

Stomach disorders, Saints Timothy and Titus, *January 26*

Students, Saint Catherine of Alexandria, *November 25;* Saint Thomas Aquinas, *January 28*

Surgeons, Saints Cosmas and Damian, *September 26;* Saint Luke, *October 18*

T

Tailors, Saint Homobonus, *November 13*

Taxi drivers, Saint Fiacre, *August 30*

Teachers, Saint Gregory the Great, *September 3;* Saint John Baptist de La Salle, *April 7*

Teenagers, Saint Aloysius Gonzaga, *June 21;* Saint Maria Goretti, *July 6*

Telecommunications, Gabriel (Michael, Gabriel, and Raphael), *September 29*

Television, Saint Clare, *August 11*

Theologians, Saint Alphonsus Liguori, *August 1;* Saint Augustine of Hippo, *August 28*

Throat ailments, Saint Blase, *February 3*

Toothache, Saint Apollonia, *February 9*

Travelers, Anthony of Padua, *June 13*

U

Undertakers, Saint Joseph of Arimathea, *August 31;* Saint Dismis, *March 25;* Saint Nicodemus, *March 17*

V

Venereal disease, Saint Fiacre, *August 30*

Veterinarians, Saint Eligius, *December 1*

Vocations, Saint Alphonsus Liguori, *August 1*

W

Waiters, waitresses, Saint Martha, *July 29*

Widows, Saint Frances of Rome, *March 9;* Saint Paula, *January 26*

Women in labor, Saints Ann and Joachim, *July 26;* Saint Elmo, *June 2*

Workers, Saint Joseph, *March 19*

Writers, Saint Francis de Sales, *January 24*

Y

Youth, Saint Aloysius Gonzaga, *June 21;* Saint Maria Goretti, *July 6;* Saint John Bosco, *January 31;* Saint Anthony of Padua, *June 13;* Saint Nicholas, *December 6;* Saint Joseph, *March 19;* Saint Raphael, *September 29*

Catholic Terms and Definitions

abortion. The deliberate termination of a pregnancy by killing the unborn child. The Roman Catholic Church considers such direct abortion a grave contradiction of the moral law and a crime against human life.

absolution. An essential part of the Sacrament of Penance and Reconciliation in which the priest pardons the sins of the person confessing, in the name of God and the Church.

abstinence. The avoidance of a particular kind of food as an act of penance or spiritual discipline; in Catholicism, the avoidance of meat on certain days.

Act of Contrition. A prayer of sorrow for one's sins, a promise to make things right, and a commitment to avoid those things that lead to sin. Such a prayer can be said anytime, but is always part of the Sacrament of Penance and Reconciliation.

adoration. The prayerful acknowledgment that God is God and Creator of all that is.

adultery. Sexual activity between two persons, at least one of whom is married to another. Prohibited by the Sixth Commandment.

Advent. The four-week liturgical season during which Christians prepare themselves for the celebration of Christmas.

almsgiving. Freely giving money or material goods to a person who is needy. It may be an act of penance or of Christian charity.

amen. A Hebrew word meaning "let it be so" or "let it be done." As a conclusion to prayer, it represents the agreement by the person praying to what has been said in the prayer.

angel. Based on a word meaning "messenger," a personal and immortal creature, with intelligence and free will, who constantly glorifies God and serves as a messenger of God to humans in order to carry out God's saving plan.

annulment. A declaration by the Church that although a civil and emotional relationship existed between a couple, no sacramental bond took place at the time of the wedding. Once a declaration of nullity (annulment) has been granted, one or both parties are free to marry again in the Church.

Annunciation. The biblical event in which the angel Gabriel visits the virgin Mary and announces that she is to be the mother of the Savior.

Anointing of the Sick. One of the Seven Sacraments, sometimes formerly known as "the Sacrament of the Dying," in which a gravely ill, aging, or dying person is anointed by the priest and prayed over by him and attending believers. One need not be dying to receive the Sacrament.

Apostles. The general term *apostle* means "one who is sent," and can be used in reference to any missionary of the Church during the New Testament period. In reference to the twelve companions chosen by Jesus, also known as "the Twelve," the term refers to those special witnesses of Jesus on whose ministry the early Church was built, and whose successors are the bishops.

apostolic fathers. A group of Greek Christian authors in the late first and early second centuries. They are our chief source of information about the early Church, and may have historical connections to the Apostles.

apostolic succession. The uninterrupted passing on of authority from the Apostles directly to all bishops. It is accomplished through the laying on of hands when a bishop is ordained.

Apostolic Tradition. *See* Tradition.

apparition. An appearance to people on Earth of a heavenly being—Christ, Mary, an angel, or a saint. The New Testament includes stories of multiple apparitions by Jesus between Easter and his Ascension into Heaven.

arms race. The competition between nations to build up stockpiles of weapons of all kinds, including weapons of mass destruction. Many of these stockpiles are large enough to destroy the world several times over.

artificial insemination. The process by which a man's sperm and a woman's egg are united in a manner other than natural sexual intercourse. In the narrowest sense, it means injecting sperm into a woman's cervical canal. The Church considers it morally wrong because it separates intercourse from the act of procreation.

Ascension. The "going up" into Heaven of the risen Christ forty days after his Resurrection.

assembly. Also known as a congregation, it is a community of believers gathered for worship as the Body of Christ.

Assumption of Mary. The dogma that recognizes that the body of the Blessed Virgin Mary was taken directly to Heaven after her life on Earth had ended.

atheist; atheism. One who denies the existence of God; and the denial of the existence of God.

Baptism. The first of the Seven Sacraments, by which one becomes a member of the Church and a new creature in Christ; the first of the three Sacraments of initiation, the others being Confirmation and the Eucharist.

Baptism of blood. The Catholic Church's firm conviction that someone who dies for the faith without being baptized actually receives Baptism through his or her death.

Beatitudes. The teachings of Jesus during the Sermon on the Mount in which he describes the actions and attitudes that should characterize Christians, and by which one can discover genuine meaning and happiness.

benediction. In general, another name for a blessing prayer. For Catholics, it more often refers to the prayer in which the Blessed Sacrament is used to bless the people.

Bible. The collection of Christian sacred writings, or Scriptures, accepted by the Church as inspired by God, and composed of the Old and New Testaments.

bishop. Based on a word for "overseer," one who has received the fullness of the Sacrament of Holy Orders, is a member of the "college" of bishops, and is recognized as a successor of the Apostles. When he serves as head of a diocese, he is often referred to as the ordinary or local bishop.

blasphemy. Speaking, acting, or thinking about God in a way that is irreverent, mocking, or offensive. It is a sin against the Second Commandment.

Blessed Sacrament. Another name for the Eucharist, especially for the consecrated bread and wine when they are reserved in the tabernacle for adoration or for distribution to the sick.

blessing. A prayer asking that God care for a particular person, place, or activity. A simple blessing is usually made with the sign of the cross.

Body of Christ. A term which when capitalized designates Jesus' body in the Eucharist, or the entire Church, which is also referred to as the Mystical Body of Christ.

breviary. A prayer book that contains the prayers for the Liturgy of the Hours.

brothers. *See* religious life; congregation; order.

calumny. Ruining the reputation of another person by lying or spreading rumors. It is also called slander, and is a sin against the Eighth Commandment.

canon. This word has a variety of meanings. The canon of the Scriptures refers to the Church's list of books of the Bible. The canon of the Mass is another name for the Eucharistic prayer. Canon law is the official body of laws for Catholics.

canonization. The official proclamation by the Pope that a deceased member of the Church is to be recognized as a saint and may serve as a model of the Christian ideal for all believers; also the name of the process by which one is found worthy of such recognition.

capital punishment. Another name for the death penalty, a sentence sometimes given to people who commit serious crimes. The Church teaches that the necessity for capital punishment in today's world is rare.

cardinal virtues. Based on the Latin word for "pivot," four virtues that are viewed as pivotal or essential for full Christian living: prudence, justice, fortitude, and temperance.

catechesis. Based on a word meaning "to echo," the process of education and formation of Christians of all ages, by which they are taught the essentials of Christian doctrine and are formed as disciples of Jesus. Those who serve as ministers of catechesis are called catechists.

catechism. A popular summary, usually in book form, of Catholic doctrine about faith and morals and commonly intended for use within programs of formal catechesis. The official and most authoritative Catholic catechism is the *Catechism of the Catholic Church.*

catechumen. One who is preparing for full initiation into the Catholic Church by engaging in formal study, reflection, and prayer.

catechumenate. The name of the full process, as well as of one formal stage within the process, by which persons are prepared for full initiation into the Church. The process is commonly reserved for adult converts to Catholicism.

cathedral. Based on a word for "chair," the official Church of the bishop of a diocese, at which he is recognized as the chief pastor. The bishop's "chair" symbolizes his teaching and governing authority within the diocese.

Catholic Church. The name given to the universal group of Christian communities that is in communion with the Pope, the successor of Peter. It was established by Christ on the foundation of his Apostles.

celebrant. The person who oversees any act of public worship. In a Eucharistic Liturgy or Mass, the celebrant is always an ordained priest.

celibacy. The state or condition of those who have chosen or taken vows to remain unmarried in order to devote themselves entirely to service of the Church and the Kingdom of God. (*See also* vow(s).)

charism. A special gift or grace of the Holy Spirit given to an individual Christian or a community, commonly for the benefit and building up of the entire Church.

charity. The theological virtue by which we love God above all things and, out of that love of God, love our neighbor as ourselves.

chastity. The virtue by which people are able successfully and healthfully to integrate their sexuality into their total person; recognized as one of the fruits of the Holy Spirit. Also, one of the vows of the religious life.

chief priests. In biblical Judaism, the priests (descendants of the tribe of Levi) were responsible for the proclamation of God's will, the interpretation of the Law, and worship and ritual sacrifice in the synagogues. Jesus often found himself in conflict with them.

chrism. Perfumed oil, consecrated by the bishop, which is used for special anointings in Baptism, Confirmation, and Holy Orders. It signifies the gift of the Holy Spirit.

Christ. *See* Jesus Christ.

Christmas. The feast day on which Christians celebrate the birth of Jesus; also refers to the liturgical season that immediately follows Christmas Day.

church. In common Christian usage, the term *church* is used in three related ways: (1) the entire People of God throughout the world; (2) the diocese, which is also known as the local church; and (3) the assembly of believers gathered for celebration of the liturgy, especially the Eucharist. In the creed, the Church is recognized as one, holy, catholic, and apostolic—traits that together are referred to as "marks of the Church."

civil authorities. The people in society who are responsible for making and enforcing civil laws. They have a responsibility for safeguarding human freedom and human dignity.

civil disobedience. Deliberate refusal to obey a law prescribed by the state, usually on moral grounds.

civil laws. The laws that govern society. Civil laws should reflect the natural law God has placed in every human heart.

clergy. In the Catholic Church, the term refers to men who receive the Sacrament of Holy Orders as deacons, priests, or bishops. In the broader Church, the term refers to anyone ordained for ministry.

college of bishops. The assembly of bishops, headed by the Pope, that holds the teaching authority and responsibility in the Church.

commandments. In general, a norm or guide for moral behavior; commonly, the Ten Commandments given by God to Moses. Jesus summarized all the commandments within the twofold or Great Commandments to love God and neighbor.

common good. Social conditions that allow all citizens of the earth, individuals and families, to meet basic needs and achieve fulfillment.

Communion of Saints. The spiritual union of all those who believe in Christ and have been redeemed, including both those who have died and those who are still living.

Concluding Rites. The final part of the liturgy, comprising a Final Blessing and the Dismissal.

concupiscence. The tendency of all human beings toward sin, as a result of Original Sin.

confession, private. Telling one's sins to a priest. It is an essential element of the Sacrament of Penance and Reconciliation.

confidentiality. Keeping safe a truth that must not be shared with others because to do so would be immoral or illegal.

confirmand. A candidate for the Sacrament of Confirmation.

Confirmation. With Baptism and the Eucharist, one of the three Sacraments of initiation. Through an outpouring of special gifts of the Holy Spirit, Confirmation completes the grace of Baptism by confirming or "sealing" the baptized person's union with Christ and by equipping that person for active participation in the life of the Church.

congregation. *See* assembly.

conscience. The "interior voice" of a person, a God-given internal sense of what is morally wrong or right. Conscience leads people to understand themselves as responsible for their actions, and prompts them to do good and avoid evil. To make good judgments, one needs to have a well-formed conscience.

conscientious objection. Refusal to join the military or take part in a war, based on moral or religious grounds. Conscientious objectors must seek official approval of their status from the government.

consecrated life. A state of life recognized by the official Church in which a person publicly professes vows of poverty, chastity, and obedience.

Consecration. Making a person (candidate for ordination), place (a new church), or thing (bread and wine) holy. During the Mass the term refers to that point in the Eucharistic Prayer when the priest recites Jesus' words of institution, changing the bread and wine into the Body and Blood of Christ.

contemplation. A form of wordless prayer in which one is fully focused on the presence of God; sometimes defined as "resting in God," a deep sense of loving adoration of God.

contraception. The deliberate attempt to interfere with the creation of new life as a result of sexual intercourse. It is considered morally wrong by the Church, which teaches that a married couple must remain open to procreation whenever they engage in sexual intercourse.

conversion. A profound change of heart, turning away from sin and toward God.

council of the Church. An official assembly of Church leaders, often for the purpose of discernment and decision making about particular issues. When represented by and concerned with the entire Church, it is called *ecumenical,* from a word meaning "the whole wide world." Councils can also be regional or local.

covenant. In general, a solemn agreement between human beings or between God and a human being in which mutual commitments are recognized; also called a testament. In the Bible two covenants are central: (1) the Covenant between God and the ancient people of Israel established in God's Sinai Covenant with Moses; also called the Old Testament or Old Covenant; and (2) the New Covenant established by Jesus through his sacrificial death and Resurrection; also called the New Testament. The term *testament* has come to be associated primarily with the Sacred Scriptures that record the history and meaning of the two biblical covenants.

Creation. The beginning of all that exists as a result of an act of God, who made everything from nothing. The story of Creation is told in the Book of Genesis.

Creator. A title given to God to signify that God and only God is the ultimate creator of everything that is and everything that ever will be.

creed. An official profession of faith, usually prepared and presented by a council of the Church and used in the Church's liturgy. Based on the Latin *credo,* meaning "I believe," the two most familiar Catholic creeds are the Apostles' Creed and the Nicene Creed.

deacon; diaconate. The third degree or level of the Sacrament of Holy Orders, after that of bishop and priest. Deacons are ordained to assist priests and bishops in a variety of ministries. Some are ordained deacons as one stage of their preparation for eventual priesthood. Others do not seek priesthood but commit to lifelong ministry to the Church. The latter are known as permanent deacons.

Decalogue. Another name for the Ten Commandments. Also called the Law or the Law of Moses.

denomination. A group of religious organizations uniting under a single legal and administrative body and subscribing to the same creed and moral code.

detraction. Revealing something about another person that is true but is harmful to his or her reputation.

devil; demon. A fallen angel, one created naturally good but who sinned against God by refusing to accept God's Reign. The term *devil* refers to Satan, Lucifer, or the Evil One, the chief of the fallen angels; *demon* refers to an agent of the Evil One.

diocesan priest. A man ordained by the bishop for service to the local Church in parish ministry or another diocesan apostolate.

diocese. Also known as a "particular" or "local" Church, the regional community of believers, who commonly gather in parishes, under the leadership of a bishop. At times a diocese is determined not on the basis of geography but on the basis of language or culture.

discernment. From a Latin word meaning "to separate or to distinguish between," it is the practice of listening for God's call in our lives and distinguishing between good and bad choices.

disciple. A follower of Christ. Based on a word for "pupil" or "student," used to designate both those who learned from and followed Jesus in New Testament times (the disciples) as well as those who commit to follow him today.

disposition. An inner attitude and readiness to receiving God's gifts (graces), particularly through the Sacraments.

doctrine. An official teaching of the Church.

dogma. Those truths that are recognized as divinely revealed, defined by the Magisterium, and accorded the fullest weight and authority. (*See also* heresy.)

domestic church. Another name for the first and most fundamental community of faith: the family.

doxology. A prayer of glory and praise to one God in three Divine Persons. Two examples of doxologies from the Mass are the Glory to God and the words that precede the great Amen.

Easter. The day on which Christians celebrate Jesus' Resurrection from the dead; considered the most holy of all days and the climax of the Church's liturgical year. (*See also* Triduum.)

ecumenical council. A gathering of all Catholic bishops, convened by the Pope and under his authority and guidance. The last ecumenical council was Vatican II, called by Pope John XXIII in 1962.

ecumenism. The movement to restore unity among the Christian Churches and, ultimately, of all humans throughout "the whole wide world" (the literal meaning of the word).

efficacious. The power something holds to cause a desired effect. The Sacraments are efficacious in bringing about the spiritual reality they signify.

embezzlement. The sin of taking funds that are not yours, from a business, an organization, or the government.

encyclical. A letter written by the Pope and sent to the whole Church and, at times, beyond the Church to the whole world; commonly focused on Church teaching regarding a particular issue or currently important matter.

envy. Jealousy, resentment, or sadness because of another person's good fortune. It is one of the capital sins and contrary to the Tenth Commandment.

Eucharist, the. Also called the Mass or Lord's Supper, and based on a word for "thanksgiving," the central Christian liturgical celebration; established by Jesus at the Last Supper. In the Eucharist, the sacrificial death and Resurrection of Jesus is both remembered ("Do this in memory of me") and renewed ("This is my Body which will be given up for you"). The Sunday celebration of the Eucharist is considered the heart of the Church's life and worship, and participation in it is expected of all Catholics of the age and ability to do so.

Eucharistic adoration. A type of prayer in which one meditates before the Blessed Sacrament, either privately or during a communal prayer such as Benediction.

Eucharistic Prayer. The part of the Mass that includes the Consecration of the bread and wine. It begins with the Preface and concludes with the people's Amen.

euthanasia. A direct action, or a deliberate lack of action, that causes the death of a handicapped, sick, or dying person. Some attempt to justify it as an act of mercy intended to relieve suffering, but the Catholic Church rejects that position, and considers euthanasia a violation of the Fifth Commandment against killing.

evangelist. Based on a word for "good news," in general, anyone who actively works to spread the Gospel of Jesus; more commonly and specifically, one of the persons traditionally recognized as authors of the four Gospels: Matthew, Mark, Luke, and John.

evangelization. The proclamation of the Gospel of Jesus through word and witness.

examination of conscience; examen. Prayerful reflection on and assessment of one's own words, attitudes, and actions in light of the Gospel of Jesus; more specifically, the conscious evaluation of one's life in preparation for reception of the Sacrament of Penance and Reconciliation.

exorcism. A power given to the Church, in the name of Jesus Christ, to free or protect a person or object from the power of the devil.

exposition. As part of Eucharistic adoration, exposition is the custom of taking the Eucharist from the tabernacle and placing it in a special vessel called a monstrance, designed to hold a host and "expose" it—that is, to make it visible—so that people can pray before it.

faith. In general, the belief in the existence of God. For Christians, the gift of God by which one freely accepts God's full Revelation in Jesus Christ. It is a matter of both the head (acceptance of Church teaching regarding the Revelation of God) and the heart (love of God and neighbor as a response to God's first loving us); also, one of the three theological virtues.

fall, the. Also called the fall from grace, the biblical revelation about the origins of sin and evil in the world, expressed figuratively in the story of Adam and Eve in Genesis. (See also Original Sin.)

fasting. Refraining from food and drink as an act of spiritual discipline or as an expression of sorrow for sin; sometimes required by the Church, especially during the liturgical season of Lent.

Father. The name for God used most commonly by Jesus and, therefore, held in high esteem by the Church. (*See also* Trinity.)

Final Judgment. The judgment of the human race by Jesus Christ at his second coming, as noted in the Nicene Creed. It is also called the Last Judgment.

first Friday. A particular devotion to the sacred heart of Jesus that involves receiving the Eucharist on nine consecutive first Fridays of the month. According to Tradition those who do so will receive special graces.

fornication. Sexual intercourse between a man and a woman who are not married. It is morally wrong to engage in intercourse before marriage, and it is a sin against the Sixth Commandment.

fortitude. Also called strength or courage, the virtue that enables one to maintain sound moral judgment and behavior in the face of difficulties and challenges; one of the four Cardinal Virtues.

forty hours' devotion. A three-day period of worship of the Blessed Sacrament, approximately equaling the time Jesus lay in the tomb. The Blessed Sacrament is exposed in a monstrance during this time.

free will. The gift from God that allows human beings to choose from among various actions, for which we are held accountable. It is the basis for moral responsibility.

fruits of the Holy Spirit. The characteristics and qualities of those who allow themselves to be guided by the Holy Spirit. They are listed in Galatians 5:22–23.

fundamentalism. An interpretation of the Bible and Christian doctrine based on the literal meaning of the words and without regard to the historical setting in which the writings or teachings were first developed; the person who holds such a perspective is called a fundamentalist.

genetic engineering. Manipulating the genetic code of plants, animals, or human beings to alter it in some way. Such activity with human DNA is considered a violation of the sanctity of life.

genuflection. Kneeling on one knee as a sign of reverence for the Blessed Sacrament.

gifts of the Holy Spirit. Special graces given to us by the Holy Spirit to help us respond to God's call to holiness. The list of seven gifts is derived from Isaiah 11:1–3.

God. The infinite and Divine Being recognized as the Source and Creator of all that exists. (*See also* Trinity.)

Gospel. Most basically, "the good news" (the phrase on which the word *gospel* is based) of the Revelation of God in and through Jesus Christ, proclaimed initially by him, then by the Apostles, and now by the Church; also refers to those four books of the New Testament that focus on the person, life, teachings, death, and Resurrection of Jesus.

grace. The free and undeserved gift of God's loving and active presence in the universe and in our lives. (*See also* sanctifying grace.)

healing, Sacraments of. The two Sacraments that are concerned with healing the mind, body, and spirit: the Sacrament of Anointing of the Sick and the Sacrament of Penance and Reconciliation.

Heaven. Traditionally, the dwelling place of God and the saints, meaning all who are saved; more accurately, not a place but a state of eternal life and union with God, in which one experiences full happiness and the satisfaction of the deepest human longings.

hell. The state of permanent separation from God, reserved for those who freely and consciously choose to reject God to the very end of their lives.

heresy. The conscious and deliberate rejection of a dogma of the Church. (*See also* doctrine; dogma.)

hierarchy. In general, the line of authority in the Church; more narrowly, the Pope and bishops, as successors of the Apostles, in their authoritative role as leaders of the Church. (*See also* Magisterium.)

Holy Communion. Another name for the Eucharist, the Body and Blood of Jesus Christ.

holy days of obligation. Feast days in the liturgical year on which, in addition to Sundays, Catholics are obliged to participate in the Eucharist.

Holy Orders. The Sacrament by which members of the Church are ordained for permanent ministry in the Church as bishops, priests, or deacons.

Holy Spirit. The third Person of the Blessed Trinity, understood as the perfect love between God the Father and the Son, Jesus Christ, who inspires, guides, and sanctifies the life of believers. (*See also* Trinity.)

holy water. Blessed water used in ritual sprinklings or when making the sign of the cross as a reminder of Baptism.

Holy Week. In the Church's liturgical year, the week preceding Easter, beginning with Palm Sunday; it culminates the annual celebration of Christ's Passion, death, and Resurrection.

homosexuality. A sexual attraction to members of one's own gender. The Church teaches that homosexual activity is morally wrong.

hope. The theological virtue by which we trust in the promises of God and expect from God both eternal life and the grace we need to attain it; the conviction that God's grace is at work in the world and that the Kingdom of God established by and through Jesus Christ is becoming realized through the workings of the Holy Spirit among us.

human dignity. The idea that because all people are created in God's image, they have fundamental worth. This notion is the foundation of Catholic social teaching.

human rights. The basic political, social, and economic rights that every human being claims, by virtue of their human dignity as beings created by God. Society cannot grant these rights and must not violate them.

humility. The virtue by which one understands that one is totally dependent on God, and also appreciates and uses properly the gifts she or he has been given by God.

idolatry. Worship of other beings, creatures, or material goods in a way that is fitting for God alone. It is a violation of the First Commandment.

Ignatian Gospel contemplation. A prayer form that uses the imagination to immerse a person in a story from the Scriptures, in order to better understand the story's meaning.

Immaculate Conception. The Catholic dogma that the Blessed Virgin Mary was free from sin from the first moment of her conception.

immortality. The quality or state of unending, everlasting life; the Catholic doctrine that the human soul survives the death of the body and remains in existence, to be reunited with the body at the final resurrection; identified in the creed as belief in "the resurrection of the body and life everlasting."

Incarnation. Based on words meaning "in flesh," the mystery and Church dogma that the Son of God assumed human nature and "became flesh" in the person of Jesus of Nazareth. The Incarnation means that Jesus, the Son of God and second Person of the Trinity, is *both* fully God and fully man.

indissolubility. A property of the Sacrament of Matrimony that excludes any possibility for breaking the marital bond.

inerrancy. The fact that the books of the Scriptures are free from error regarding the spiritual and religious truth that God wishes to reveal through them for the sake of our salvation. (*See also* inspiration, biblical.)

infallibility; infallible. The gift of the Spirit to the whole Church by which the leaders of the Church—the Pope and the bishops in union with him—are protected from fundamental error when formulating a specific teaching on a matter of faith and morals.

initiation. The process by which a nonbaptized person is prepared to become a full member of the Church. The three Sacraments of initiation are Baptism, Confirmation, and the Eucharist.

inspiration, biblical. The guidance of the Holy Spirit in the development of the Scriptures, whereby the Spirit guided the human authors to teach without error those truths of God that are necessary for our salvation. It is on the basis of inspiration that we can call the Bible the Word of God.

intercession. A prayer on behalf of another person or group.

Introductory Rites. The opening of the liturgy designed to prepare the assembly for the celebration. It consists of the Entrance Chant, Greeting, Penitential Act, Kyrie, Gloria, and the Opening Prayer (Collect).

in vitro fertilization. The fertilization of a woman's ovum (egg) with a man's sperm outside of her body. The fertilized egg is transferred to the woman's uterus. The process is considered to be a moral violation of the dignity of procreation.

Islam. Founded by the prophet Muhammad, it is one of the three great religions of the Western world, with connections to both Judaism and Christianity. It's holy scriptures are gathered in the Qur'an.

Israelites. The Chosen People of God; members of the twelve tribes descended from Jacob who inhabited the land of Israel during biblical times.

Jesus Christ. The Son of God, the second person of the Trinity, who took on flesh in Jesus of Nazareth. *Jesus* in Hebrew means "God saves," and was the name given the historical Jesus at the Annunciation. *Christ,* based on the word for "Messiah," meaning "the anointed one," is a title that was given Jesus by the Church after his full identity was revealed.

Judaism. The religious practices, beliefs, perspectives, and philosophies of the Jewish people. The biblical roots are in the Hebrew Scriptures, particularly in the Torah (which is also the first five books of the Bible). The Jews also have a rich wisdom tradition handed down to them from their rabbis (teachers).

justice. The Cardinal Virtue concerned with rights and duties within relationships; the commitment, as well as the actions and attitudes that flow from the commitment, to ensure that all persons—particularly the poor and oppressed—receive what is due them.

justification. God's act of bringing a sinful human being into right relationship with him. It involves removal of sin and the gift of God's sanctifying grace to renew holiness.

just war. War involves many evils, no matter the circumstances. For a war to be just, it must be declared by a lawful authority, and there must be just cause, the right intention (such as self-defense), and weapons must be used in a way that protects the lives of innocent people.

Kingdom of God. The reign or rule of God over the hearts of people and, as a consequence of that, the development of a new social order based on unconditional love. Also called the Reign of God.

Kyrie Eleison. Greek for "Lord, have mercy." The short prayer, along with its counterpart, *Christe Eleison,* "Christ, have mercy," is part of the Penitential Act at the beginning of a Eucharistic Liturgy.

laity. All members of the Church, with the exception of those who are ordained. The laity share in Christ's role as priest, prophet, and king, witnessing to God's love and power in the world.

Last Supper. A supper during the Jewish celebration of Passover that was the last meal Jesus shared with his disciples before being handed over for crucifixion. It is remembered by Catholics as the occasion of the first Eucharist, and is commemorated by believers on Holy Thursday.

Law, the. *See* New Law; Old Law.

lectio divina. A form of meditative prayer, usually focused on a passage from the Scriptures, that involves repetitive readings and periods of reflection; can serve as either private or communal prayer.

lectionary. The official liturgical book from which the readings selected for the Liturgy of the Word during Mass are proclaimed. The person who proclaims the Word is called a lector.

legitimate defense. The teaching that limited violence is morally acceptable in defending yourself or your nation from an attack.

Lent. The liturgical season of forty days that begins with Ash Wednesday and ends with the celebration of the Paschal mystery in the Easter Triduum, the season during which believers focus on penance for sin.

liturgical celebration. *See* liturgy.

liturgical year. The annual cycle of religious feasts and seasons that forms the context for the Church's worship.

liturgist. One who has the training and responsibility for planning and coordinating all aspects of the worship life of a faith community.

liturgy. Based on a word meaning "public work," the official public worship of the Church, the heart and high point—or source and goal—of which is the Eucharist.

Liturgy of the Eucharist. The second major part of the Mass, it comprises the Presentation and Preparation of the gifts, the Prayer over the Offerings, the Eucharistic Prayer, and the Communion Rite.

Liturgy of the Hours. The official, nonsacramental daily prayer of the Catholic Church. The prayer provides standard prayers, Scripture readings, and reflections at regular hours throughout the day. (See also breviary.)

Liturgy of the Word. The first major part of the Mass, it comprises three scriptural readings, a Responsorial psalm, a homily, the Nicene Creed, and petitions.

living wage. Also called just wage, it is a fair payment that a worker receives from an employer, which allows the wage earner and his or her family to live a life of dignity and meet basic needs.

Lord. The Old Testament name for God that in speaking or reading aloud was automatically substituted for the name Yahweh, which was considered too sacred to be spoken; in the New Testament, used for God the Father and for Jesus Christ, to reflect awareness of Jesus' divine identity as the Son of God.

Lord's Prayer. Another name for the Our Father.

love. The human longing for God and a selfless commitment to supporting the dignity and humanity of all people, simply because they are created in God's image. Also called "charity," it is one of the three theological virtues.

lust. Intense and uncontrolled desire for sexual pleasure. It is one of the seven Capital Sins.

Magisterium. The name given the official teaching authority of the Church, whose task is to interpret and preserve the truths of the Church revealed in both the Scriptures and Tradition.

Magnificat. Mary's prayer of praise when she visited her cousin Elizabeth. It is recorded in Luke 1:46–55. The name of the prayer is the first word of the prayer in Latin, which means "magnify."

marks of the Church. The four characteristics of the true Church of Jesus Christ: one, holy, catholic (universal), and apostolic. These marks are recited at Mass as part of the Nicene Creed.

marriage; Matrimony. Marriage is an exclusive, permanent, and lifelong contract between a man and a woman in which they commit to care for each other and to procreate and raise children; when the marriage takes place between baptized persons who enter into a covenant modeled on that between Christ and the Church, it is recognized as the Sacrament of Matrimony. The two terms are often interchanged.

martyr. A person who voluntarily suffers death because of her or his beliefs. The Church has canonized many martyrs as saints.

Mary. The mother of Jesus, sometimes called the Blessed Virgin Mary. Because Jesus is the Son of God and the second Person of the Trinity, Mary is also given the title Mother of God.

Mass. Another name for the Eucharist. Based on the Latin word *missa,* meaning "to be sent," refers to the Dismissal, in which worshipers are told to "Go in peace, glorifying the Lord by your life."

masturbation. Self-manipulation of one's sexual organs for the purpose of erotic pleasure or to achieve orgasm. The Church considers masturbation to be a sin because the act cannot result in the creation of a new life. It is also wrong because it is self-serving, and God created sex not for self-gratification but to unify a husband and wife in marriage.

meditation. A form of prayer involving a variety of methods and techniques, in which one engages the mind, imagination, and emotions in order to focus on a particular truth, biblical theme, or other spiritual matter.

ministry. Based on a word for "service," in a general sense any service offered to help the Church fulfill its mission; more narrowly, particular expressions of such service (e.g., the ministry of catechesis and liturgical ministries).

miracle. A special manifestation, or sign, of the presence and power of God active in human history.

modesty. From the same root word as "moderation," it means keeping one's attitudes, actions, speech, dress, and other behaviors controlled in a way that acknowledges one's own dignity.

monotheism. Belief in one God instead of many.

monstrance. The special vessel designed to hold a host and make it visible for Eucharistic adoration.

morality. Dealing with the goodness or evil of human acts, attitudes, and values; involves matters such as right judgment, decision-making skills, personal freedom and responsibility, and so on.

mortal sin. An action so contrary to the will of God that it results in a complete separation from God and God's grace. As a consequence of that separation, the person is condemned to eternal death. To be a mortal sin requires three conditions: it must involve grave matter, the person must have full knowledge of the evil of the act, and the person must give his or her full consent in committing the act.

mystagogy. In general, post-baptismal catechesis intended to more fully initiate people into the mystery of Christ. It is also the name of the final period in the catechumenate.

mysticism. An intense experience of the presence and power of God, resulting in a deeper sense of union with God; those who regularly experience such union are called mystics.

natural law. Our God-given instinct to be in right relationship with God, other people, the world, and ourselves. The basis for natural law is our participation in God's wisdom and goodness because we are created in divine likeness. The fundamental expressions of natural law remain fixed and unchanging, which is why natural law is the foundation for both personal morality and civil norms.

New Law. The law of the Gospel of Jesus Christ, it is a law of love, grace, and freedom. The New Law fulfills and perfects the Old Law, or the Law of Moses.

New Testament. The twenty-seven books of the Bible written during the early years of the Church in response to the life, mission, death, and Resurrection of Jesus; also, another name for the New Covenant established between God and humanity by Jesus.

Nicene Creed. The formal statement or profession of faith commonly recited during the Eucharist. (*See also* creed.)

novena. From the Latin word for "nine," it is a public or private devotion that extends for a period of nine days. In some cases a novena is offered on a designated day for nine weeks or nine months.

nuns. *See* religious life; congregation; order.

obedience. Based on a word meaning "to hear or listen," the willingness and commitment to submit to the will of God, as well as to Church teachings and practices that reflect the will of God. (*See also* vow(s).)

oil of the sick. The oil used in the Sacrament of the Anointing of the Sick. It is blessed by the bishop along with other holy oils during the annual chrism Mass.

Old Law. The Law of Moses, summarized by the Ten Commandments. The Old Law is the first stage of revealed law, in preparation for the Gospel.

Old Testament. The forty-six books of the Bible that record the history of salvation from Creation, through the story of ancient Israel, and up to the time of Jesus; also refers to the Old Covenant established between God and the people of Israel in God's encounter with Moses on Mount Sinai.

ordained ministers. Those who have received the Sacrament of Holy Orders—that is, deacons, priests, and bishops.

Ordinary Time. The time in the liturgical year that is not part of a special season like Advent, Christmas, Lent, or Easter.

ordination. *See* Holy Orders.

Original Sin. The sin by which the first humans disobeyed God and thereby lost their original holiness and became subject to death. Original Sin is transmitted to every person born into the world. (*See also* fall, the.)

papacy. The name given the office and authority of the Bishop of Rome, the Pope. As the successor of Saint Peter, the Pope serves as both a symbol and an agent of the unity of all believers.

parable. A story intended to convey a religious truth or particular teaching through the use of metaphors; a central feature of Jesus' teaching ministry.

Paraclete. A name for the Holy Spirit, based on a word for "helper" or "advocate."

parish. A specific community of believers, commonly but not always defined geographically, whose pastoral and spiritual care is guided by a priest or other leader appointed by a bishop.

Parousia, Christ's. The second coming of Christ, when his Kingdom will be fully established and his triumph over evil will be complete.

Paschal lamb. A name for Jesus, whose death and Resurrection redeemed humanity. The name is associated with Passover, a commemoration of the deliverance of the Jewish people from Egypt. To avoid the slaughter of firstborn sons by the Egyptian army, the Jews sprinkled the blood of a lamb on their doorposts.

Paschal mystery. The term given the entire process of God's plan of salvation by which God redeemed humanity from sin in and through Jesus' life, death, Resurrection, and Ascension into glory. Christians enter into the Paschal mystery through sacramental initiation, and they participate in it by faithfully living out the process of dying and rising that characterizes all life.

Passion, the. The suffering and death of Jesus.

pastoral. Refers to the daily life of the Church, especially as it takes place at parish and diocesan levels. Based on a word for "shepherd" or "shepherding," the person who tends to the pastoral care of a community is commonly called the pastor.

penance. In general, an attitude of the heart in which one experiences regret for past sin and commits to a change in behavior or attitudes; particular acts of penance may include the practice of spiritual disciplines such as prayer or fasting, or participation in the Sacrament of Penance and Reconciliation.

penance, communal. The Sacrament of Penance and Reconciliation celebrated within a gathering of a faith community. The most common form includes opportunities for individual confession and absolution.

Penance and Reconciliation, Sacrament of. One of the Seven Sacraments of the Church, the liturgical celebration of God's forgiveness of sin, through which the sinner is reconciled with both God and the Church.

Pentecost. The biblical event following the Resurrection and Ascension of Jesus at which the Holy Spirit was poured out on his disciples; the first Pentecost is often identified as the birth of the Church. In the Christian liturgical year, the feast fifty days after Easter on which the biblical event of Pentecost is recalled and celebrated.

People of God. The biblical image for the Church. Those who share in Christ's mission as priest, prophet, and king.

perjury. The sin of lying while under an oath to tell the truth.

permanent deacon. *See* deacon; diaconate.

petition. A prayer form in which one asks God for help and forgiveness.

Pharisees. A Jewish sect during the time of Jesus known for their strict adherence to the Law and their concern with superficial matters.

plagiarism. Using another person's thoughts, creative ideas, writings, music, and so forth without permission, and presenting them as one's own. It is a form of stealing and is a sin against the Seventh Commandment.

polygamy. Having more than one spouse. It is contrary to the sanctity of marriage.

Pope. Based on a word for "father," the successor of Saint Peter and Bishop of Rome, who holds the office of the papacy. Often called the Holy Father.

pornography. A written description or visual portrayal of a person or action that is created or viewed with the intention of stimulating sexual feelings.

poverty. As a social reality, indeed, a social sin, a condition of material need experienced by the poor. The Church, in imitation of Jesus, expresses its central concern for the poor through its commitment to justice. As an attitude and value, a spirit of detachment from material things and a commitment to share all that one has with those who have not.

praise. A prayer of acknowledgment that God is God, giving God glory not for what he does, but simply because he is.

prayer. The lifting of mind and heart to God in praise, petition, thanksgiving, and intercession; communication with God in a relationship of love.

precepts of the Church. Sometimes called the commandments of the Church, these are obligations for all Catholics that are dictated by the laws of the Church.

preferential love. A moral obligation for individuals and for the Church that requires special attention to those who are poor, considering their needs first and above all others.

presbyter. A term used for officials in the early Church. Today it is an alternative word for "priest."

priest; priesthood. The second of three degrees or "orders" in the Sacrament of Holy Orders, along with bishop and deacon. The priest is called to serve the community of faith and its members by representing and assisting the bishop in teaching, governing, and presiding over the community's worship. Priests generally minister within a parish, school, or other setting within a diocese.

priesthood of the faithful. The belief that the Body of Christ is made up of priestly people who share in Christ's royal priesthood.

prostration. A prayer posture in which a person lies stretched out on the ground, face down, as a sign of adoration, submission, and humility. This posture is part of the rite of ordination.

prudence. The virtue by which a person is inclined toward choosing the moral good and avoiding evil; sometimes called the rudder virtue, because it helps steer the person through complex moral situations; related to conscience, and one of the four Cardinal Virtues.

purgatory. A state of final purification or cleansing, which one may need to enter following death and before entry into Heaven.

reason. The natural ability human beings have to know and understand truth.

Reconciliation. *See* Penance and Reconciliation, Sacrament of.

redemption; Redeemer. The process by which we are "bought back" (the meaning of *redeem*) from slavery to sin into a right relationship with God. We are redeemed by the grace of God and through the life, death, and Resurrection of Jesus Christ. As the agent of redemption, Jesus is called the Redeemer.

Reign of God. *See* Kingdom of God.

religion. The beliefs and practices followed by those committed to the Gospel of Jesus and full participation in the life of the Church. By virtue of the First Commandment, the first duty of a religious person is to worship and serve God alone.

religious life; congregation; order. A permanent state of life and an organized group of Christians, recognized by the Church, who have taken vows to live in community and to observe the disciplines of poverty, chastity, and obedience. Religious men are often called brothers, monks, or friars; religious women, sisters or nuns.

religious priests. Priests who are ordained within a religious community for service to the community and its ministries. With the permission of the local bishop, they may also lead parishes within a diocese.

religious vows. The vows, or promises, made by a person who becomes a full member of a religious community. Traditionally there are three vows: poverty, chastity, and obedience.

reparation. Making amends for something one did wrong that caused harm to another person or led to loss.

repentance. An attitude of sorrow for a sin committed and a resolution not to sin again. It is a response to God's gracious love and forgiveness.

restitution. Making things right with another person or people who have been harmed by an injustice, or returning or replacing what rightfully belongs to another.

Resurrection, the. The passage of Jesus from death to life "on the third day" after his Crucifixion; the heart of the Paschal mystery, and the basis of our hope in the resurrection of the dead. (*See also* resurrection of the dead.)

resurrection of the dead. The Christian dogma that all those deemed righteous by God will be raised and will live forever with God in Heaven; the conviction that not only our souls but also our transformed bodies will live on after death ("I believe in the resurrection of the body"). (*See also* resurrection, the.)

Revelation. God's self-communication and disclosure of the divine plan to humankind through creation, events, persons, and, most fully, in Jesus Christ.

ritual. The established form of the words and actions for a ceremony that is repeated often. The actions often have a symbolic meaning, such as the anointing with chrism at Confirmation.

rosary. A popular devotion to Mary, the Mother of God.

Sabbath. In the Old Testament, the "seventh day" on which God rested after the work of Creation was completed; in Jewish Law, the weekly day of rest to remember God's work through private prayer, communal worship, and spiritual disciplines such as fasting; for Catholics, Sunday, the day on which Jesus was raised, which we are to observe with participation in the Eucharist in fulfillment of the commandment to "keep holy the Sabbath."

Sacrament. In Catholic life and worship, the seven efficacious signs of God's grace, instituted by Christ and entrusted to the Church, by which divine life is dispensed to us.

sacramental character. A permanent and indelible spiritual mark on a person's soul, sealed by the Holy Spirit as a result of Baptism, Confirmation, and Holy Orders. For this reason these Sacraments cannot be repeated.

sacramentals. Sacred signs (such as holy water and a crucifix) that bear some resemblance to the Sacraments, but which do not carry the guarantee of God's grace associated with the Seven Sacraments.

Sacraments at the service of communion. The name given to the two sacraments that are directed toward building up the People of God, namely Holy Orders and Matrimony.

Sacraments of healing. *See* healing, Sacraments of.

Sacraments of initiation. *See* initiation.

sacrilege. An offense against God. It is the abuse of a person, place, or thing dedicated to God and the worship of God.

saint. Someone who has been transformed by the grace of Christ and who resides in full union with God in Heaven. (*See also* canonization; Communion of Saints.)

salvation. Liberation from sin and eternal union with God in Heaven. Salvation is accomplished by God alone through the Paschal mystery—the dying and rising of Jesus Christ.

salvation history. The pattern of events in human history that exemplify God's presence and saving actions. In Catholic thought *all* of history is salvation history, even though God's presence may not be recognized.

sanctifying grace. A supernatural gift of God by which our sins are forgiven and we are made holy. It restores our friendship with God.

scandal. An action or attitude—or the failure to act—that leads another person into sin.

scribes. In Jewish history these were government officials and scholars of the Law of Moses. They enforced the requirements of the Law.

Scripture(s). Generally, the term for any sacred writing. For Christians the Old and New Testaments that make up the Bible and are recognized as the Word of God.

simony. Buying or selling of something spiritual, such as a grace, a Sacrament, or a relic. It violates the honor of God.

sin. Any deliberate offense, in thought, word, or deed, against the will of God.

sisters. *See* religious life; congregation; order.

slander. Injuring another person's reputation by telling lies and spreading rumors. It is also called calumny.

social doctrine. The body of teaching by the Church on economic and social matters that includes moral judgments and demands for action in favor of those being harmed.

social encyclical. A letter from the Pope addressed to members of the universal Church regarding topics related to social justice, human rights, and peace.

social justice. The Church's commitment, and mandate to its members, to engage in conscious efforts to fight against, if not overcome, social sin.

social sin. The collective effect of sin over time, which corrupts society and its institutions by creating "structures of sin." Examples of social sin are racism, sexism, and institutionalized poverty.

society. A broad part of the human community that is distinguished by common values, traditions, standards of living, or conduct.

solidarity. Union of one's heart and mind with those who are poor or powerless, or who face an injustice. It is an act of Christian charity.

Son of God. Title frequently applied to Jesus Christ, which recognizes him as the second Person of the Blessed Trinity.

soul. The spiritual life principle of human beings that survives after death.

spirituality. In general, the values, actions, attitudes, and behaviors that characterize a person's relationship with God and others. For Christians a life guided by the Holy Spirit, lived out within the community of believers, and characterized by faith, hope, love, and service.

stewardship. An attitude that we do not own the gifts God has given us, but are trustees of those gifts. We have an obligation to share our time, talent, and material treasures with others.

suicide. Deliberately taking one's own life. It is a serious violation of God's Law and plan. It is usually accomplished as a result of serious mental and emotional anguish, and in such cases is not considered a free and deliberate act.

superstition. Attributing to someone or something else a power that belongs to God alone, and relying on such powers rather than trusting in God. It is a sin against the First Commandment.

symbol. An object or action that points us to another reality. It leads us to look beyond our senses to consider the deeper mystery.

tabernacle. The receptacle in a church in which the consecrated bread and wine of the Eucharist is reserved for Communion for the sick and dying; sometimes the focus of private and communal prayer and adoration.

temperance. The Cardinal Virtue by which one moderates her or his appetites and passions in order to achieve balance in the use of created goods.

temptations. Invitations or enticements to commit an unwise or immoral act that often include a promise of a reward, to make the immoral act seem more appealing.

thanksgiving. A prayer of gratitude for the gift of life and the gifts of life.

theological virtues. The name for the God-given virtues of faith, hope, and love. These virtues enable us to know God as God and lead us to union with God in mind and heart.

theology. Literally, the study of God; the academic discipline and effort to understand, interpret, and order our experience of God and Christian faith; classically defined as "faith seeking understanding."

Theotokos. Greek for "God-bearer." It is the name given to Mary after an ecumenical council in the fifth century to affirm that she is the mother of the human Jesus and the mother of God.

Tradition. This word (from the Latin, meaning "to hand on") refers to the process of passing on the Gospel message. Tradition, which began with the oral communication of the Gospel by the Apostles, was written down in the Scriptures, is handed down and lived out in the life of the Church, and is interpreted by the Magisterium under the guidance of the Holy Spirit.

transubstantiation. In the Sacrament of the Eucharist, this is the name given to the action of changing the bread and wine into the Body and Blood of Jesus Christ.

Triduum. The three days of the liturgical year that begin with the Mass of the Lord's Supper on Holy Thursday and end with evening prayer on Easter Sunday.

Trinity. Often referred to as the Blessed Trinity, the central Christian mystery and dogma that there is one God in three Persons: Father, Son, and Holy Spirit.

venerate. An action that shows deep reverence for something sacred. For example, on Good Friday, individuals in the assembly venerate the cross by bowing before or kissing the cross.

venial sin. A less serious offense against the will of God that diminishes one's personal character and weakens but does not rupture one's relationship with God. (*See also* mortal sin.)

vice. A practice or a habit that leads a person to sin.

vigil for the deceased. Another name for "wake service." It is a prayer service that takes place before a funeral, to pray for the repose of the soul of the deceased and for strength for those who grieve the loss.

virginal conception and birth. The dogma that Jesus was conceived in the womb of Mary and born by the power of the Holy Spirit and without the cooperation of a human father. (*Note:* This is not to be confused with the Immaculate Conception of Mary.)

virtue. A good habit, one that creates within us a kind of inner readiness or attraction to move toward or accomplish moral good. The theological virtues are faith, hope, and love.

vocal prayer. A prayer that is spoken aloud or silently, such as the Lord's Prayer. It is one of the three expressions of prayer, the other two being meditation and contemplation.

vocation. A call from God to all members of the Church to embrace a life of holiness. Specifically, it refers to a call to live the holy life as an ordained minister, as a vowed religious (sister or brother), in a Christian marriage, or in single life.

vow(s). A free and conscious commitment made to other persons (as in marriage), to the Church, or to God. Religious vows—those taken by members of religious congregations or orders—commonly include poverty, chastity, and obedience.

wake service. *See* vigil for the deceased.

way of the cross. A religious devotion or exercise modeled on Jesus' Passion—his trial, walk toward his death on the cross, and burial in the tomb. Sometimes called the stations of the cross, the devotion involves meditation on each step in Jesus' journey.

worship. Adoration of God, usually expressed publicly in the Church's official liturgy as well as through other prayers and devotions.

Yahweh. The Old Testament name for God, frequently translated as "I am who I am."

Acknowledgments

The scriptural quotations contained herein are from the New Revised Standard Version of the Bible, Catholic Edition. Copyright © 1993 and 1989 by the Division of Christian Education of the National Council of the Churches of Christ in the United States of America. All rights reserved.

The prayers, devotions, beliefs, and practices contained herein have been verified against authoritative sources.

The section "Patron Saints and Their Causes" on pages 34–42 is adapted and quoted from the American Catholic Web site, *www.americancatholic.org/Features/Saints/patrons.asp*, accessed March 12, 2008. Used with permission of St. Anthony Messenger Press.

To view copyright terms and conditions for Internet materials cited here, log on to the home pages for the referenced Web sites.

During this book's preparation, all citations, facts, figures, names, addresses, telephone numbers, Internet URLs, and other pieces of information cited within were verified for accuracy. The authors and Saint Mary's Press staff have made every attempt to reference current and valid sources, but we cannot guarantee the content of any source, and we are not responsible for any changes that may have occurred since our verification. If you find an error in, or have a question or concern about, any of the information or sources listed within, please contact Saint Mary's Press.